Anonymous

Echoes of holy thoughts

Arranged as private meditiations before a first communion

Anonymous

Echoes of holy thoughts
Arranged as private meditiations before a first communion

ISBN/EAN: 9783337281595

Printed in Europe, USA, Canada, Australia, Japan

Cover: Foto ©Lupo / pixelio.de

More available books at **www.hansebooks.com**

Echoes of Holy Thoughts:

ARRANGED AS

PRIVATE MEDITATIONS

BEFORE A

FIRST COMMUNION.

Second Edition.

WITH A PREFACE BY THE

REV. JOHN HAMILTON THOM.

"Looking unto Jesus, the author and finisher of our faith."
HEBREWS xii. 2.

WILLIAMS AND NORGATE,

14, HENRIETTA STREET, COVENT GARDEN, LONDON:
AND 20, SOUTH FREDERICK STREET, EDINBURGH.

1872.

CONTENTS.

b

PREFACE.

THE Publishers desire a name; the Author, professing only to give " Echoes," will not speak in her own voice ; and so I am asked to write some words of Preface to a second edition of this little book. Perhaps without being out of harmony with the simple freshness of these Meditations, or losing sight of the tenderness of their application to the feelings and the wants of a first Communion, I may attempt briefly to answer the deep question—How is it possible for material symbolism to have permanent connection with a spiritual Religion, and to be a help, not an injury, to the " spirit and truth " which are its notes of universality?

"This is my Body which is given for you: this do in remembrance of Me."—" This cup is the new testament in my Blood, which is shed for you."—The words broke suddenly out of the moved heart of Christ ; the grandest of those unpremeditated inspirations which enable the deepest natures to connect the intense life of the spirit with whatever representative things the scene and the hour supply. To suppose that there was aught else in our Lord's thoughts than to make the most of the emergencies of the time, to communicate through a symbol sure to grow in expressiveness something of the fellowship of His own life with God, something of its meaning, something of its power, to the feeble, unspiritual men who on the morrow were to be left without their Leader, with His Gospel in their keeping,—is not only to impair the naturalness of this monumental Act, but also gravely to mistake the whole genius of Christianity. It is of the essence of the religion of the Son of God, that it fills the soul with the spirit of our Father, and trusts that spirit to make or find its own occasions. The water of Baptism, the bread and wine of the Eucharist, of the Communion, of the Sacramental vow of discipleship, are *inexhaustible* symbols, because, like the spiritual emblems and parables of Nature, of the mountains or of the seasons, they transcend all limitations of present feeling, and cannot be reduced to any final form of words. They are for ever new, and suggestive of what is new, to kindled souls that are brought within the currents of inspiration. We lose the wonderful power of the Lord's Supper if we do not enter into the emo-

tions of Christ in the moment of the in-
spired act, and feel in it the divine energy of
spiritual genius—we know how unworthy
are these words, but we have no other—
kindling a soul within the Twelve to meet
the present need,—and using, as the fittest
for His purpose, a universal Language,
capable for ever of conveying more and
more of its immeasurable significance to
the universal Church.

The ordinary occasions which urge dying
men to place those who are to come after
them in trust with an interest or commission
of God's, afford but a faint image of the
necessity that pressed upon the dying
Christ, *then or never*, to put the spirit of
His own being into forms of expression and
appeal which memory and familiar custom
would for ever be reproducing, and His
death and their own great experiences
would for ever be interpreting. " With de-

sire have I desired to eat this passover with you before I suffer." He compressed the sum of His life in God,—love, holiness, truth, with their inevitable cost,—into the emblems the occasion offered : symbols of spiritual nourishment and symbols of martyrdom blend before Him into one, for the strength of our life is that for which we will lay down our life ; our meat and our drink is to do the will of our Father ; the bread of life is obedience unto death ; the measure of our being is the measure of our love when tested by endurance ; " This is my body, broken for you": and from that hour to the disciples of every age these elements have spoken of a spiritual fellowship that cannot be broken, though flesh and heart should fail,—of a Faith equal to any hiding of our Father's face,—of Love and Obedience as the substance and the sustenance of being,—of the true Life which thinks only of holiness and truth, and accepts any sacrifices that meet us on a way in which we are walking with God. The exalted spirit Christ, in His ecstasy of inspiration, poured this whole meaning into a symbol naturally presented which He knew for the Twelve would for ever be recurring ; and the heart of mankind, with more or less of simplicity and fidelity, has ever since adopted the Emblem and its meaning. This is the whole spiritual significance of the Lord's Supper.

Nor was this symbolism a solitary instance of its kind. There were other acts of monumental utterance, in those last days, which show how impending death was inciting Him to leave, through pregnant images, indelible expressions of Himself. He spoke, as in a soliloquy, of the mysterious law of spiritual reproduction : "Unless a corn of wheat fall into the ground and die,

it abideth alone ; but if it die, it bringeth
forth much fruit." He marked the barren
fig-tree, and made it impossible for any
follower of His to pass that familiar way
without thinking of an unfruitful life, of
abused privileges and coming judgment.
He knelt at the disciples' feet, He, Master
and Lord, and sculptured the new lesson
of Love, that he is the greatest who is most
the servant of all. The costly ointment
poured upon His head He pronounced to be
no waste, for it had the odour of death and
served for His embalming. It was a gracious
deed done to Him who was all Grace,—and
the due offerings of our hearts must go up
as well to God who has everything, as to
the poor who have nothing ; and this, too,
by His wonderful Word, He took within
those monumental acts which remain to all
ages, inexhaustible emblems of His spirit :
" Wheresoever this gospel shall be preached

in the whole world, there shall also this, that this woman hath done, be told for a memorial of her." And so the Last Supper is but the intensest of a series of kindred utterances. To His eye, so rapt, yet so clear, the only Bread of Life is the Love that will give itself to be broken in self-sacrifice, the Body of our works,—the only Wine that nourishes is the Spirit of our Father flowing as life-blood in us. And such a stamp of reality does He impress upon these suggestions of the moment, in the height of His inspiration, that they continue to emit His mind for ever, like the natural symbols of God's Spirit. Truly never man spake like this man : for His words become things, and do not pass away.

Thenceforwards the disciples felt that the spirit of the life of Christ, breathing from these emblems, was their only bond of union

in God, for and against the World. And
so mightily significant was the memorial
office, so full did they find it of the power
and peace of the Master, that they renewed
its inspiration as often as they met together,
the earthen vessels of a heavenly treasure,
with nothing to sustain them but the light
of the knowledge of the glory of God
shining in the face of Christ. Their only
security was never to fall away from those
great remembrances, lest alone and unsup-
ported they should wither like branches
that abide not in the vine.—And though
for *us* the world has changed, and persecu-
tion and sufferance have ceased, and the
once dishonoured Cross is now the emblem
of all that is sacred or is dear, worn reve-
rently on the banner and the breast, still
the shadows of our Discipline are terrible as
before to impatient worldliness,—clouds and
darkness are still beneath God's feet,—Piety

is of faith not of sight,—earthly Love can rejoice only in trembling, knowing that Death
walks by its side,—Mercy still makes its
rounds with bleeding feet, feeling the Holy
Spirit only in the undying charity that cannot stop the evil against which it strives, so
that to the blind earth the pity might seem
all supplied by man, the trial and the agony
by God;—and thus the great symbols of
faithfulness unto death, of light in darkness,
of love laying down its life because it will
not break the fellowship which alone *is*
Life, have never lost their meaning, and
cannot be outgrown. Here at least is
Christian antiquity, a tradition from the
primitive times, a succession which goes
back to the Apostles, from the multitudes
which no man can number to the Guest-
Chamber where Christ sat with the Twelve,
and all of them were weak, and one of them
was a traitor.

We take simply the human view of this
question ; we do not presume to speak, or
that any one can speak, in the name of an
authoritative commandment, which all are
bound on their allegiance implicitly to
obey; such commands are reserved for
those great matters which carry with them
their own universal authority, which no
soul can refuse and not deny itself :—we
ask for what *spiritual* reason must we drop
a link that connects us with the church of
the Crucified, with the past generations of
those who have lived and died in the faith
of the Son of God ? We speak not of
ordinances, of the efficacy of sacraments,
of positive institutions as the channels of
Grace,—God forbid,—we are Christ's free-
men, children of the same Father, and spirit
to spirit is the Law of Life ;—but of expressive acts now instinct with their first significance, employed by Christ because in no

other way could He adequately represent
His great meaning, and which represent it
still. What form of *words* could *grow* in
the power of conveying the sense of union
with our Lord, of one Life for us all, of one
Discipline for us all, as children of one Father who perfects through suffering? The
Emblems have two aspects ;—as symbols of
Communion, we eat of the same bread ; we
drink of the same cup ; we have but one
source of spiritual nourishment ; we are all
branches in the vine which draws its life
from God : as symbols of Obedience, of
fidelity unto death through all tests of
self-sacrifice,—the Body is broken ; flesh
and soul are parted ; the Wine is turned to
Blood.

It is true that our spiritual fellowship
does not depend upon the symbols which
express it, even as natural symbols do not
make the spiritual realities of which they

are the vehicles. But why, in peril of our souls, as we all are, from vague sentiments and floating ideals which have no tendency to embody themselves, should we consent to lose the vivid help of an expressive Act, which, towards the delineation and imitation of our Lord, may become to us as a finely cutting chisel in a sculptor's hand? Especially, why should not the Lord of Life still speak to the *young* in the same Language by which He sought to infuse a strength not their own into hearts that were in a like case, only beginning to be spiritually born, weak, passionate, and tempted? Dangers are around them; powers of evil are working in their nature; a sudden infirmity might place the great gulph of sin between them and the unstained time that then never could return: and is it not well to use definite safeguards, —to enter into covenant with their God,

—to exact solemn pledges from their own hearts,—to take the great sacramental vow of our youth, the vow of purity, to resist the passions and the world,—to see in the symbols of Communion the beauty of holiness, with the cost of conflict,—and, as with their hands upon the Cross, to place the dedication of their lives, and the image of their Lord, between them and temptation!

J. H. T.

ECHOES OF HOLY THOUGHTS.

CHAPTER I.

THE CHOICE.

E cannot remember our first thought of God, nor our first prayer to Him. We have been taught to speak to Him as our Father, and to learn of Him from Christ our Lord. But to all of us there comes a time when the sense of our moral responsibility is brought vividly before us. We are standing at the entrance of life, and must henceforth depend less upon the guidance of

I

those to whose care God has committed our youth, and more upon the dictates of our own consciences. We look back upon a childhood marked by many faults and many efforts, full of enjoyment and of love, shadowed by some troubles and vexations, and sanctified, perhaps, by some first sorrow which has revealed to us a new meaning in life. We look forward to the necessity of doing our work in the world. We are taking our lives into our own hands for good or for evil. We are gradually, but surely, crossing the border land where for a moment we are standing, and soon the turmoil of the world and the noise of work may deaden the music of the Spirit that speaks to us in this first sense of responsibility. Let us therefore pause now, and try to understand the meaning of the life God has given to us.

The solemn words come ringing in our ears as they came to the Israelites of old, "Choose ye this day whom ye will serve."

The God whose strong right arm has brought us through the unknown dangers of our early years—whose Providence has led us through the desert where we knew of no path for ourselves, and has fed and clothed us without effort of our own, even as He sent manna from heaven in the wilderness—shall we serve Him? Or shall we turn to the gods of the nations among whom we may be thrown? Shall we serve the idols we can so easily create, and worship our own ease, our self-indulgence, our worldliness, our ambition, our pride, in one word, *ourselves?*

And even as the Jewish people answered, so, with all solemnity and earnestness, looking down upon the fair land of promise lying before us, do we answer, " We will serve the Lord!" How can we hesitate? Has He not been ever with us? We will serve Him! But let us remember that this choice is no light one. It is not to be made one hour and forgotten the next ;

held securely as long as no difficulties or perplexities come with it ; but cast aside as soon as we find it easier to follow the ways of others or our own self-will. If we will rally round the standard of our King, and enroll ourselves as soldiers in the army of the Lord, we must remember that the battle is not soon over ; that the conflict between good and evil can never cease ; but that unto our life's end we are to resist the evil and choose the good, and wait patiently till in His own good time God shall give the victory.

In the Christian Church, from the first ages, the formation of this choice has been marked by the setting aside of a time for reflection and meditation ; for the gaining of some true self-knowledge ; for earnest thought and careful consideration ; so that we may not rush forward unarmed, to be overthrown at the first onset. And then the Choice of Good has been consecrated by some religious ceremony, whereby we

may set the seal to this dedication of ourselves to God and to His Christ. Can we
find any better means of expressing our
hearty desire to consecrate ourselves to
God, than by obeying the command of our
Lord Jesus Christ, and joining at His Table
in keeping the memory of His life and of
His death? Hereby we name ourselves His
disciples, and manifest our desire to follow
Him—if God calls us—even unto death.
This is the rite by which the Christian
Church has always recognised the choice,
and consecrated the desire, of all young
disciples to be, not their own, but "Christ's,
and Christ is God's." Let us then try to
prepare ourselves that we may partake of
the Lord's Supper, and that God's blessing
may rest upon us, and be with us.

O Holy Father, be with us now, and
teach us. We would come to Thee to know
our own weakness and to find Thy strength.
Keep us from rashness and self-conceit.
Show us our sins, O Lord, but give us Thy

Grace to leave them. We pray for pure
hearts and earnest minds, so that we may
seek Thee heartily, and become Thy children more truly than we have been, by
bearing more likeness to Thy beloved Son.
In His name, and as His disciples, O our
Father, we pray Thee now to bless us.
Amen.

Heavenly Father! to whose eye
Future things unfolded lie ;
Through the desert, where I stray,
Let Thy counsels guide my way.

Lead me not, for flesh is frail,
Where fierce trials would assail ;
Leave me not, in darkened hour,
To withstand the tempter's power.

Help Thy servant to maintain
A profession free from stain ;
That my sole reproach may be
Following Christ, and fearing Thee.

Lord! uphold me day by day ;
Shed a light upon my way ;
Guide me through perplexing snares ;
Care for me in all my cares.

Should Thy wisdom, Lord, decree
Trials long and sharp for me,
Pain or sorrow, care or shame,
Father ! glorify Thy name.

Let me neither faint nor fear,
Feeling still that Thou art near ;
In the course my Saviour trod,
Tending still to Thee, my God.

Conder.

CHAPTER II.

WHAT DOES OUR CHOICE MEAN?

BEFORE we thus solemnly bind upon ourselves this choice of good and not evil, let us look at some of the difficulties which have already hindered us, and with which we know we must still contend. What has hitherto prevented our "being good," though we have tried over and over again? We have all some knowledge of our besetting sins, and have often struggled hard against them. Yet, just after our most earnest resolutions and our most fervent prayers, we have yielded to them more easily than ever. Dare we think that the same shall

not be the case now? What are we to do?
Can we take upon ourselves Christ's name,
and pledge ourselves to be His disciples,
when we know that we are so weak?

Let us trust much less in ourselves and
much more in God. It is true that we cannot come to God for help and blessing
while we still love and cherish our sins.
We must learn to see them as He sees
them, and then we shall hate and desire to
leave them. But if we turn to God heartily
and repent, if we bring our sins into the
light of His Presence and see their shame-
fulness, He will be with us and help us.
When we have once felt His real and living
Presence, when we have had experience that
" even as a father pitieth his children, so the
Lord pitieth us," when we have learnt to
love Him and desire Him above all things,
then we cannot help longing to be what He
wishes to have us; and though we fall again
and again, though we sin the same sins and
yield to the old temptations, we feel a thrill

of shame and sorrow such as we have never known before. We hate the sin ; we almost hate ourselves, that after all that God has done for us, we could forsake Him and grieve Him. And as we take refuge in the Sanctuary of His Presence, we ask Him to save us from ourselves, and not to leave us alone in our weakness and wilfulness. This is very different from the cold, careless mood, in which sometimes we hardly seem to care whether we do right or wrong, and drift on in the old accustomed ways, yielding to our common faults, and not seeing much harm in them. From this sleep— this death of the soul—we must pray that God will deliver us, and by letting us know and love Him, teach us to know ourselves.

We may find that this waking up to a true sense of sin leads us through a time of great trouble and darkness, but we must not be dismayed though sometimes we feel almost hopeless of making any progress.

For the promise of help has been given
to us. "If God be for us, who can be
against us?" We know that God will help
us to be good, and will save those whose
desire is towards Him, somehow, some-
time, either in this world or in the next.
He will not let one of His little ones perish ;
so we will come to Him ; and casting our
burdens upon Him, we shall find strength
to bear them, and courage to serve Him,
and Him alone.

How shall we know what this true service
of God really is ? Thanks be to God, who
hath sent His Son into the world, that who-
soever believeth in Him, might have life !
Christ has shown us what it means to be a
Child of God. "Believing in Christ" does
not mean merely giving our assent to the
facts told in the Gospels, or to any theories
founded upon them ; but it means, living
according to His Spirit ; so we must learn
of Him and follow Him. The Spirit of
God, which tells us when we sin, and guides

our weakest efforts, "without whom nothing
is good, nothing is holy," was *in* Christ, so
that in Him we have the revelation of God
to man.   God gives us to-day, not laws or
rules, definite and binding upon all alike,
but He asks us to receive His Holy Spirit
and to live,—each of us according to his
special character and his appointed place,—
in the faith and after the example of Christ
our Lord.   Therefore we must learn from
Christ, and study His life as of the deepest
interest to us.   How can we live according
to His example if we do not know what it
is ?   How can we be His, unless we have
learnt to love Him ?   Thus only can we
know what God requires of us in His
service.

O God, help us and make us Thine.
Give us Thy light that we may know our
sins ; Thy grace that we may leave them.
Without Thee, we can do no good thing.
Enlighten our eyes that we may behold
Thine image in Thy Son.   Give us Thy

Holy Spirit, that we may learn of Christ, and be Thine, as Christ is Thine. Amen.

> Father ! reveal Thy Son in me,
>   To my soul's eye unclouded ;
> The fulness of Thy deity,
>   In mortal semblance shrouded,
> When, for a name o'er every name,
> He bore the cross, despised the shame,
>   And rose,—the world's Redeemer.
>
> All things for Him, may I forsake,
>   In poverty and weakness ;
> His gentle burden on me take,
>   And wear His yoke with meekness :
> So shall I find in labour, rest,
> In suffering, peace—of Christ possessed,
>   In me the hope of glory.
>
> *Montgomery.*

CHAPTER III.

CHRIST OUR LIFE.

E have read the story of our Lord's Life in the Gospels again and again, but now we turn to it with a new interest. Since we are to take Christ for our Master, we must listen to His words. We are to take Him for our Example, so we must look at Him and watch Him. We are to follow in His footsteps, so we must see where they are leading us. We are to live the same life, for His "life is the light of men," therefore we must try to understand the spirit and meaning of that life. We must, each for ourselves, study thus the character

of our Lord, and, as we read, try to bring
our own lives before the light of His life.
Let us not only read what He did when
He was here amongst us, but try so to
enter into the motive of His actions, that we
may know what He would have us to do in
the present time. Let us now take one or
two examples of this manner of studying
Christ's life.

When He was only twelve years old He
lingered behind in the Temple, that He
might be about His Father's business.
Already He forecast His high mission, and
had its weight upon His heart. Yet He
went back to His village home, and was
obedient to His parents till He was thirty
years of age. To those whom God had
placed over Him, Christ was subject, knowing that thus He was fulfilling His Father's
will. He waited, and worked, and watched,
until He should be called by God to more
public service. Have we not felt the longing to do some great work, to fill some im-

portant place, to be of some great use?
Do we not sometimes fret because, like
children, we are still kept in obedience?
We say we can judge best for ourselves;
we believe we can do some better work—
" for God," we think—but perhaps after all
it is only our own self-conceit that we in-
tend to serve; we do not like to realise that
we are not trained and fitted yet for high
and noble service, and we would rather
follow our own desire of self-assertion than
wait till we are distinctly called of God.
But surely this fact, the only one we know
of our Lord's youth, has been told in vain,
unless it teach us that to many, and often
to those upon whom He will bestow the
most, God sends first a long time of wait-
ing, and of training, of ordinary duty, and
of quiet home life; and if we can find no
way of serving God in our homes, how
shall we dare to think that we are fit to
serve Him in the world?

All through His life, we find our Lord

quietly doing, day by day, the work that lay before Him, whatever it might be. He seemed to have no rule but to do His Father's will. He felt the anointing of the Lord, He knew He was sent "to preach the gospel to the poor, to heal the broken-hearted, to preach deliverance to the captives, and recovering of sight to the blind, to set at liberty them that are bruised, to preach the acceptable year of the Lord ;" and He did it, never hasting, never resting, never turning aside to other thoughts, never neglecting any occasion that came before Him, and never caring for Himself at all. He might have been rich, and great, and powerful ; He might have been a king and won His country back from the Roman yoke ; He might have been His nation's idol, but He *was* poor and despised, and scorned, and neglected, until after only three years of earnest, but ill-requited toil, He completed the self-sacrifice of His life, by His death. We,

2

His young disciples, are called only to
common duties ; we have to fill our place
in the ordinary life around us.   Can we do
it in His spirit ?   Can we do whatever
comes to our hand, because it is the Will
of God for us, and so do nothing upon
which we cannot feel His blessing?   Can
we go on quietly though the world pass us
by, caring only for the eye of God, and
nothing at all for our position among men,
while yet we are ready to take up and
perform   earnestly, whatever new duties
gradually come into our lives?   Can we
learn our Lord's spirit of self-sacrifice, and
forgetting ourselves, remember only to love
God and our fellow-men ?

We are longing to be Christ's disciples in
deed and in truth, and not in name only, and
He says to us, " Are ye able to drink of the
cup that I shall drink of, and to be baptized
with the baptism that I am baptized with?"
Dare we answer as did the disciples of old,
" We are able ? "   If so, let us remember

His solemn warning, that thus they must
do, if they desired to follow Him ; and
that the service and the sacrifice must be
rendered unto God in singleness of heart,
without any looking for reward or expectation of future greatness. Not for Himself
did Christ live and work and suffer and
die ; and not for the hope of any future
happiness must we follow in His steps, but
only because we love God, and desire His
Will before our own.

We see our Lord gentle, and tender, and
sympathising, helping all who came near
Him, comforting all who mourned ; yet
brave to rebuke evil, strong to suffer, willing
to die. We hear Him blessing the meek,
the pure in heart, the peace-makers, the
merciful, the seekers after righteousness ;
and we would take our place among them,
and receive His blessing, too. We watch
Him as He points out those who are, indeed, His " brethren, and His sisters, and
His mother ; " and we long to be worthy

to be ranked among those "who do the.
will of My Father which is in heaven."

We follow Christ as He draws near His
death, and goes to Jerusalem to meet it,
with perfect trust in God.   He knew He
was just about to suffer all that was most
terrible, and yet as He broke the bread and
poured out the wine at that Last Supper,
He gave thanks to God.

We see Him kneeling at the feet of the
disciples, who, He knew, would so soon
desert and betray Him, and deny Him at
the moment of His utmost need.   We hear
Him telling them, that even as He loves
and serves them, they are to love and serve
one another ; and shall not we be very
thankful, when, by serving others however
humbly—by doing for them the meanest
offices of love—we know that we are following and serving our master, Christ ?

We may be called upon to bear pain or
sorrow ; but if in the midst of it we can
raise our eyes to Christ, as He hangs upon

the cross, our pain seems to fade away, by comparison with that of Him "whom, not having seen, we love;" and we are strengthened to endure our little troubles for the sake of Him who "bore our griefs, and carried our sorrows."

There is no word or act of our Lord's which is not full of deep meaning, and which does not teach us what we ought to be. Let us earnestly think of them, and learn from Him; until, in every doubt and difficulty, we can turn to Christ, and find help in the hour of our need.

O Father, teach us more and more to enter into the spirit of Thy Holy Child, Jesus. Let us learn of Him, and follow Him. May we listen to His voice, and learn the lessons which He teacheth us. May He be with us now, and show us the way, and give us meek and loving hearts to tread in it, wherever it may lead. Give us grace to hear Thy voice, and to do Thy will, even as He did,—ready to die

for Thee, when Thou requirest it of us.
Show us the beauty of Self-Sacrifice; give
us hearts to love it, and wills to endure
unto the end. So we may be His disciples
and Thy children.   Amen.

> The Son of God gave thanks
>   Before the bread He broke ;
> How high that calm devotion ranks
>   Among the words He spoke !
>
> Thanks, 'mid those troubled men ;
>   Thanks, in that dismal hour ;
> This world's dark prince advancing, then,
>   In all his rage and power.
>
> Thanks, o'er that bread's dread sign ;
>   Thanks, o'er that bitter food ;
> Thanks, o'er the cup that was not wine,
>   But sorrow, fear, and blood.
>
> And shall our griefs resent
>   What God appoints as best,
> When He, in all things innocent,
>   Was yet, in all distressed ?
>
> Shall we unthankful be
>   For all our blessings round,
> When, in that press of agony,
>   Such room for thanks He found ?

O, shame us, Lord ! whate'er
  The fortunes of our days,
If suffering, we are weak to bear ;
  If favoured, slow to praise.

Frothingham.

CHAPTER IV.

HOW CAN WE FOLLOW CHRIST?

WE study, thus, our Lord's life; and our hearts thrill with devotion, and the desire to live as He lived, and to be, in some real sense, His disciples. But we have to turn to our daily duties, and again the old trials and temptations wait for us. Let us look at some of these, in the light of that principle of love to God, and of self sacrifice, which we have seen to be the meaning of Christ's life. And, as we do this, we shall almost always find that our difficulties have their root in *self-love*. This not only interferes with the purity of our love for God

and man, but it spoils and destroys the
very talents and powers God has given for
His service. Let us "love God with all
our heart, and soul, and mind, and strength,"
and we shall have no time to think of ourselves. Then our love of God will flow
forth quite naturally, in love and service to
all around us. We shall not so much meet
and conquer every temptation that comes
to us, as learn to live on a higher level.
We must climb the mountain of devotion, till the mists and clouds lie below
us, and, in God's clear sunshine, we hardly
feel the trials which, but a little while before, seemed to hide His Face from our
sight.

What is the meaning of the quick, im-
perious temper, which suddenly flashes up
at some word or act of supposed affront,
except that our self-love has been hurt,
and we will let our neighbour know it ?
We have been supposed to be in fault,
when others have, at least, had their part

with us; and why should we bear the blame? We have a right to be considered, and no one shall forget that right; so, with ungentle look, or angry word, we retort, and nurse our indignation till it glows red hot. But suddenly the thought, "Thou, God, seest me," comes like a whisper into the heart; the passionate indignation which, only a moment ago, seemed so virtuous, changes into a shape so dark and ugly, that we cannot bear to look at it; and as, in the old legends, the evil spirit shrank away at the sight of the Cross, so does our self-love shrink away from the light of God's Presence. But we have been cherishing this love of self; we,—who would fain be Christ's soldiers to our life's end—have been harbouring an enemy! and we hardly dare to meet His eye. We, who want to love God only, have been loving ourselves! We who would strive, like Christ, to love our enemies, have been angry with our friends! and we can but ask for pardon and for help. Over and over again the same temptation comes ; but, if we are in earnest, God will not forsake us, and will help us, " as in the past fidelity of His Providence He has helped others as heavily laden as ourselves." More and more constant will be that sense of His Presence, in which sin cannot dwell ; more and more rapid will be the change from our own quick temper to the conscious-ness of sin, till, at last, the true effort will be rewarded, and, by God's help, the victory will be gained. The natural warmth of moral indignation—checked and controlled when our own self-esteem or reputation are concerned—will glow with intenser heat for God and right, and may flash forth in earnest effort to resist evil ; and this inclination, which has hitherto seemed only hurtful, will become a high and useful weapon in the armoury of God.

But it may be that we have calmer and

more placid natures. We are indifferent
to the feelings of others. They may think
and speak of us as they like, only we will
quietly go on our own way, and please ourselves. It does not matter to us what
course others may take, we are absorbed
in our own affairs; we live in a world of
fancy, perhaps, and from the midst of our
own day-dreams, look out with cold in-
difference upon the wants and wishes of
those among whom God has cast our lot.
So the hard frost of selfishness withers up
every flower in our hearts, and from our
barren gardens we can bring no garlands
of loving duty to present to our Lord.
But, like the first breath of spring, the spirit
of the life of Christ breaks in upon our
coldness, and we see the hard, and dead,
and dry condition of our lives. What have
we been doing for others? What service
have we rendered to Him who hath done
so much for us? We may have dreamed
of duty; but the simplest action, done not

for ourselves, but for the sake of others, and for the love of God, will bring with it a new life, and a sense of power greater than we have ever felt before. Yet, here too, we may turn our natural disposition into a talent for serving God; for this very power, of doing without the sympathy of others, and of pursuing our own purposes resolutely, may give us strength to fight for God, even alone and unaided, if we will train it to be His servant, and learn to use it only for His sake.

There are some of us, again, whose sense of duty to God seems deadened by the desire to be thought pleasant, and to be liked by our neighbour. We try to be agreeable, and take pains to be amusing; we are ready to accommodate ourselves to the wishes of others; we dearly love the admiration we try so hard to win; and suddenly we are startled to find that we have no higher motive. We leave undone the duties which no eye but God's can

mark ; we care for no work which others
do not praise ; we live on the surface of
life, and have no courage to undertake,
no strength to perform, any sterner work
that God may send. But we have been
wasting, and spoiling, and turning to our
own selfish ends, one of the highest talents
that God can give; and if we look at
Christ, we see how we may rightly use it.
God has given us this strong desire for
love and sympathy, that we may help and
bless others, not that we may enjoy ourselves. To comfort and cheer the hearts of
those that mourn, to encourage those who
are in despair, to bear the burdens of the
weary, to brighten the lives of the lonely,
to be a message from God to all among
whom He sends us ; this is the privilege of
those to whom God has given the love of
being loved ; this is the solemn duty and
responsibility laid upon us by His hand.
Can we fulfil it aright ? By forgetting
ourselves, and living only as His servants,

may we not follow very closely in our Lord's own footsteps?

Let us then each learn for ourselves where our danger lies, and how we can turn the old sins into new service of God, remembering always that though we can do nothing of ourselves, we " can do all things through Christ that strengtheneth " us.

O Holy Father, we have sinned and done evil in Thy sight, but we turn to Thee to help us and save us. " Create in me a clean heart, O God, renew a right spirit within me. Cast me not away from Thy presence ; take not Thy Holy Spirit from me. Restore unto me the joy of Thy Salvation, and uphold me with Thy free Spirit !" Make us faithful, O our Father, in our place and work. Teach us to forget ourselves, to forsake ourselves, that we may find Thee. Draw us very near unto Thyself, and show us how we may be Thine, and serve Thee faithfully, and love Thee

truly.   So shalt Thou give us the victory,
through Jesus Christ our Lord.   Amen.

Fight the good fight, lay hold
  Upon eternal life ;
Keep but thy shield, be bold,
  Stand through the hottest strife :
Invincible while on the field,
Thou canst not fail, unless thou yield.

No force of earth or hell,
  Though fiends with men unite,
Truth's champion can compel,
  However pressed, to flight ;
No powers of darkness in the field
Can tread thee down, unless thou yield.

Trust in thy Saviour's might ;
  Yea, till thy latest breath,
Fight, and, like Him in fight,
  By dying, conquer death ;
Invincible upon the field
Thou canst not fall unless thou yield.

Great words are these, and strong ;
  Yet, Lord, I look to Thee,
To whom alone belong
  Valour and victory ;
With Thee, my Captain in the field,
I must prevail, I cannot yield.

                              Montgomery.

CHAPTER V.

THE LORD'S SUPPER.

E HAVE tried thus far, to realise the nature of our choice, and the meaning of discipleship to Christ. Let us now turn our thoughts more directly to the rite, by which, as we have seen, all Christian Churches agree to express the solemn dedication of the whole life to God and to His Christ.

In some Churches, however, other meanings than this simple one, have become attached to the "Communion of the Lord's Supper," and have gradually changed its significance. The Roman Catholics have gathered up around it the doctrine of

3

Transubstantiation ; and they believe that the consecrated bread and wine of the Eucharist are really changed into the body and blood of our Lord ; so that the wafer eaten by the communicant is not bread, but flesh. This doctrine, strange as it seems to us, arose in part from the too literal interpretation of our Lord's words—" Take, eat ; this is my body, which is broken for you." Christ describes Himself as the bread of life, and adds : " Except ye eat the flesh of the Son of Man, and drink His blood, ye have no life in you." But, almost in the next sentence, He explains to those who murmured at so hard a saying, " It is the spirit that quickeneth, the flesh profiteth nothing ; " thus does the meaning of our Lord stand revealed in the exhaustible richness of its spiritual truth, " for the letter killeth, but the Spirit giveth life."

The Established Church, in some of its branches, denies that the bread and wine are absolutely changed into the body and blood of our Lord, but maintains that His flesh and blood are present in them, and are received by the communicant with the sacred elements to the salvation of his soul. To all members of the Church of England the Holy Communion is a mystical rite, upon which God's blessing specially rests; to neglect it, is to refuse the means of grace He has vouchsafed, and to risk the salvation of their souls. It is one of the Sacraments, without the reception of which, God has not promised to accept the most devoted service.

Many other Protestant Churches see in it only the solemn observance of our Lord's command to keep the memory of His death till He comes; but they will admit no one to that Holy Table who cannot give proof of some sudden and special conversion from sin to Grace, or show some signal mark of God's favour and Election.

But, if we would draw near His Table

in the name of Christ alone, we must seek
for the real meaning of the Lord's Supper
in the record of its origin; and try to learn
from our Lord Himself what He intended
that it should signify.

We call ourselves His disciples; let us
place ourselves in that upper chamber,
where Christ is about to eat the last Passover with His disciples: let us join the little
band that gathered round Him the evening
before He suffered. "With desire have
I desired to eat this Passover with you."
He had come to Jerusalem to die, to com-
plete the self-sacrifice of His life by His
death; and as He was consciously entering
into the shadow of death, the simplest
things and actions assumed a monumental
aspect, and acquired a new and lasting significance. The blasted fig-tree, barren when
He sought its fruit, was the type of the
nation that rejected and refused Him. The
box of ointment, broken over His feet, re-
presented the anointing of His body, for the

burying which drew so near. By outward
action did He engrave upon their hearts the
lesson of humility and brotherly love ; the
kneeling Saviour at the feet of His disciples
was the real and living example of the spirit
He would leave with them. "If I, your
Lord and Master, have washed your feet,
ye also ought to wash one another's feet."
And as He sat at supper, with His disciples,
His heart overflowing with the thought of
the coming sorrow, the very bread and
wine transfigured themselves before Him,
and in the sanctity of that hour obtained a
lasting symbolism. The broken bread
seemed to represent His body which He was
to give for them ; the wine, His blood,
which He was so soon to shed for the life
of the world. "Greater love hath no man
than this, that a man lay down his life for
his friends ;" and for us, also ; for we too
are His friends, in as far as we have any
share in His spirit.

Thus, by visible things, He expressed the

reality of the invisible ; and impressed for
ever upon the hearts of His disciples the
feelings that so strongly moved Himself.
Christ chose the moment of His most com-
plete self-sacrifice, to recall Himself most
vividly to the minds of His disciples.   A
few short hours, and the sacrifice would be
completed, and His disciples, faint-hearted
and ignorant, would be left without a guide
or master.   Before He left them, He would
fain impress upon them the meaning of His
life and death ; He bound them together
by the memory of this last evening, and
engraved Himself upon the common articles
of their daily food.   Never henceforth
should they eat bread or drink wine without
keeping the memory of this last hour with
their Lord.   Nor did the disciples ever lose
the solemn impress of that hour ; and as
often as they assembled together to break
bread, they did it in remembrance of Him.
Was it strange, that He seemed nearer to
them then than at any other time ? that

after He had parted from them, and was hidden from their sight, He should still seem most sensibly present when, with solemn hearts. they recalled that first Communion with their Lord ?

Let us, then, gather round the Table of our Lord ; so shall we keep fresh and vivid the memory of His self-sacrifice ; we shall realise His presence, draw strength and inspiration from His example, and enter into some real communion with Him whom we desire to serve. We come, not because we have learnt, but because we desire to learn ; not because we are holy, but because we love holiness, and desire to behold it, that we may love it more. We are weak, let us come to Him for strength. We are ignorant, but Christ can teach us. We are blind, but He can enlighten our eyes that we shall see. We are selfish, let us look upon Him who gave Himself for us. We are proud, but we behold Him, who made Himself of

no account. We are exacting, and we see
Him, not ministered unto, but ministering,
and among us as one that serveth. We
are rebellious and wilful, and we hear His
prayer, " Not my will, but Thine be done."
We are cold and worldly, but the sight
of His love shall warm our hearts and
draw us to the love of God. We are sinful,
but He came to call sinners to repentance,
and to heal those whose souls are sick.
We are weary and heavy laden, but He
has said, " Come unto me, all ye that
labour and are heavy laden, and I will
give you rest."

O Thou, Who hast given us Thy holy
Son to lead us unto Thee, so graft, we
pray Thee, the memory of His life, and
of His death, upon our hearts, that re-
ceiving His image in our own souls, we
may become less unworthy to be called
His disciples and Thy children. Grant
this, O God, for the love of Jesus Christ
our Lord. Amen.

According to Thy gracious word,
  In meek humility,
This will I do, my dying Lord,
  I will remember Thee.

Thy body, broken for my sake,
  My bread from heaven shall be ;
Thy testamental Cup I take,
  And thus remember Thee.

Gethsemane can I forget ?
  Or there Thy conflict see,
Thine agony and bloody sweat,
  And not remember Thee ?

When to the Cross I turn mine eyes,
  And rest on Calvary,
O lamb of God, our sacrifice !
  I must remember Thee :

Remember Thee, and all Thy pains,
  And all Thy love to me ;
Yea, while a breath, a pulse remains,
  Will I remember Thee.

And when these failing lips grow dumb,
  And mind and memory flee,
When Thou shalt in Thy kingdom come,
  Jesus, remember me.

Montgomery.

CHAPTER VI.

THE COMMUNION.

OTHER names, besides that first one of the " Lord's Supper," have been given to this service, and in each some spiritual meaning is hidden.

It is the "Sacrament:" the vow of allegiance taken by the soldier to his commander; the vow taken by us, to the captain of our salvation, whereby we express our readiness to endure hardness, as good soldiers of Jesus Christ, and to fight under His banner to our life's end. We eat of this bread, and, looking unto Christ, we see that it means, " the Bread of Life," that communion with the Father

which gave Him strength. " My meat is to
do the will of Him that sent me, and to
finish His work." " Man shall not live by
bread alone, but by every word that pro-
ceedeth out of the mouth of God." If
Christ needed this strength, this abiding
sense of communion with the Father, in
order to be able to endure until the end,
how much more do we need it, if we would
follow where He leads ? We drink of the
cup He gives us, and the wine represents to
us that spirit of self-sacrifice by which He
could lay down His life in His Father's
service. With these emblems before us,
speaking to us, as no words can speak, do
we solemnly take upon ourselves His name,
desiring to fight valiantly in His cause, so
that we may be found upon His side, and at
last be more than conquerors, through the
might of Him that loved us.

It is the "Eucharist":—the thanksgiving.
" It is very meet, right, and our bounden
duty that we should, at all times, and

in all places, give thanks unto Thee, O
Lord, Holy Father, Almighty and Ever-
lasting God ; " but especially do we give
thanks, when we meet together in remembrance of Him whom God hath given to be
our Lord and our Saviour. If Christ gave
thanks, as He brake the bread and poured
out the wine,—the emblems of the self-
sacrifice so soon to be accomplished,—shall
not we much more give thanks, for the
love wherewith God hath loved us, for the
Son whom He hath sent to be the life of
the world ? We thank Him for that perfect example, for that holy life, for that
willing death ; we thank Him for the law
of the Spirit of Life in Christ Jesus our
Lord ; and with solemn and awe-struck
hearts, we thank Him yet more, that we
are called to follow in His footsteps, to partake of His spirit, to become one with Him.
"Therefore with Angels and Archangels,
and with all the company of heaven, we
laud and magnify Thy glorious Name ;

evermore praising Thee, and saying, Holy, Holy, Holy, Lord God of Hosts, heaven and earth are full of Thy glory ; glory be to Thee, O Lord, Most High." For in this our thanksgiving we are not alone, but united with all who, in all lands and in all ages, have been led by Christ to the Mighty Help of God.

Our " Communion " with Christ leads us to a nearer communion with the Father. But we can draw near to the Father in spirit and in truth only when we acknowledge our relationship with all His children. Nothing merely personal or individual may intrude to divide our hearts from all who are the children of God, the brethren of the Lord. The Communion of Saints—the union of the one family in heaven and earth—becomes a living reality to us, as we gather round the Table of Him who hath opened the gates of eternal life. Here, as nowhere else, we find again all whom we have loved and lost—all who

have been once with us, though now we see
them no more; and we meet here all those,
living or dead, whom never having seen, we
yet have learnt to love, for their oneness of
heart with us, in common allegiance to our
Lord.   For time and death have no power
to separate those who meet around the
throne of God, and join in the one universal
hymn of praise.   All differences fade away
in the sense of the love of our One Father,
the grace and help of our Lord Jesus Christ,
and the baptism of the Holy Spirit—
whereby we may become one with God,
even as Christ is one.

O Father, speak to us, and we will hear ;
give us a deep sense of Thy Presence, and
make us Thine own in very truth.   We consecrate ourselves to Thee ; all that we are,
and all that we have, we bring to Thee and
lay upon Thine altar.   Accept us, O Father,
and sanctify this our desire to be, not our
own, but Christ's ; so shall we be Thine.
May we learn of Him, and follow Him ;

make us strong to endeavour, steadfast to labour, willing to endure. Send down the grace of Thy Holy Spirit upon us, and bless us, that not in name only, but in deed and in life, we may be the disciples of Jesus Christ our Lord. Amen.

The Faithful men of every land,
    Who Christ's own rule obey,
The holy dead of every time—
    The Church of Christ are they.

The saints who die, and leave us now,
    The good of long ago,
Women and men, and children young,
    Still living here below

Who have the same eternal hope,
    The same unceasing care,
One universal hymn of praise,
    One common voice of prayer.

Since we are members, then, of Christ,
    How holy should we be,
How faithful to obey our Head
    In truth and purity !

Since we are all made one in Him,
    How gentle should we prove,
How peaceful in our ways and words,
    How tender in our love !

So shall our Head, at all times near,
  Dwell in His members blest,
To lead us in His Church on earth
  Safe to His Church in rest !

Anon.

CHAPTER VII.

SELF CONSECRATION.

THIS Communion of the Lord's Supper is then a service of commemoration, of remembrance. But we do not remember Christ aright, if we come to watch with Him here one hour, to be near Him at the time of His great self-sacrifice, and then with forgetful hearts go back to our daily work, and live as though we had never known Him. Our remembrance of Christ is real only when it pervades and inspires our whole lives. In every perplexity and doubt, in every difficulty and duty, we may look to Him, and remembering Him, we shall find strength and inspiration.

4

It is in the times when God makes us sharers in the discipline of His Son, in the temptations, sorrows and tribulations through which He became perfect, that we are especially called to remember our communion with our Master—the times when Faith is most removed from sight, and Hope from fruition—the times when Love is least requited, and our Life in God is a life of trust, of patience, of perseverance, of forbearance, of long-suffering expectation, of joy only in the Holy Spirit.

When Duty is difficult, but plain and clear, Christ says, " Remember me : remember the emblems of our fellowship;" " If any man will be my disciple, let him take up his Cross daily and follow me."

When Duty is difficult, and the end not clear,—when the prompting of Self-Sacrifice is terrible, and the issue is uncertain, and we are tempted to doubt whether God requires it at our hands,—*then* Christ says, "Remember me:" "Now is my soul troubled, and what shall I say? Father, save me from this hour! But for this cause came I unto this hour : Father, glorify Thy name!"

When we are wearied, and would rest ; when we are tempted to think that God is all powerful, and needs not us ; that He can accomplish His own purposes, without our help ; that it is enough if we are saints in submission, without seeking to be soldiers in action, then Christ says, " Remember me :" " My Father worketh hitherto, and I work." " Whatsoever the Son seeth the Father do, those things doeth the Son likewise." " Are there not twelve hours in the day? Work whilst it is day, for the night cometh in which no man can work."

When we are involved in the shadows of our mortality—our affections and sympathies weighed down by the sense of present loss, and of the changeableness of earthly things,—then Christ says, " Re-

member Me:" "If you loved me, you would
rejoice, for I go to the Father:" "Let not
your hearts be troubled, ye believe in God,
believe also in me: in my Father's house
are many mansions."

And when the time of our own great
change is present to us,—present through
an act of forecasting thought, or present
because flesh and heart seem failing—then,
Remember the Son of Man and the Son of
God. "Peace I leave with you, *my* peace
I give unto you;"—a heart at peace with
earth and heaven,—through all injuries
forgiven, "Father, forgive them, for they
know not what they do;"—through every
earthly piety fulfilled, "Behold thy Son!
Behold thy Mother!"—through every heavenly trust unclouded, "Father, into Thy
hands I commend my spirit."

In this great commemorative act, through
these living symbols, the essence of all
our Master's being is thus presented to us,
that we may promptly summon to our

aid the Grace of Christ, in all our times of need.

Again, we renew in this Sacrament our vow of allegiance, and pledge ourselves to be Christ's soldiers and servants. But our fidelity must be tested in the warfare of the world ; and our daily life is the battle-field, where we must either conquer or yield. To suffer, to deny ourselves in His service, to let no gracious impulse pass unfulfilled, no gentle deed remain unperformed—to this we are called. We are to shrink from no danger, to be willing for any toil, to endure hardship cheerfully and bravely, if we would be good soldiers of Jesus Christ. His kingdom is not yet established upon earth ; the harvest still waits to be gathered, but the labourers are few. We look forward with earnest longing to a time of purer and of holier life ; but let us remember that we, in our place—unimportant though it may be,—by our work—feeble and insignificant though it may seem,—must help to bring it nearer. By fidelity to duty, by every act of right, by every word of truth, by each loving deed and gentle action, by every self-forgetting thought and generous impulse cherished and worked out, we are fighting for the Kingdom of our Lord. The gifts we enjoy, the talents we possess, are not our own, but God's ; to be improved and perfected and consecrated to Him. We may not neglect, nor under-estimate them, nor pass them by with false humility. Every faculty, mental, moral, or spiritual, with which God has endowed us, must be cultivated to its full extent and beauty. How can we know with which weapon God will call upon us to fight for Him ?   Only when all are bright and burnished, are we sure that we can be ready for the sudden call of duty.

We are filled with the solemn sense of Thanksgiving, as we celebrate the great Love of our Lord ; but if our hearts have caught any reflection of that love, however faint and feeble, we shall find, throughout our whole lives, the echoes of that song of praise. The sadness of alienation passes. away into the glad sense of the Presence of God. If we suffer, it is His Hand that holds the cup to our lips. If we rejoice, it is His Love which crowns us with loving-kindness. If we faint before temptation, He opens to us a way of escape. If we are able to be faithful, it is by His exceeding Grace. And, with hearts resting upon Him, we can but give thanks for all His mercies.

Thus, led by the Spirit of Christ up to the Throne of God, we draw near to Him in our sorrow, trouble, or temptation; in our work, our duty, and our effort; in our trust, our joy, our peace; and find our true life in the presence of our Father; and our communion with Him shall fill, not one brief hour, but our whole existence.

The thoughts and aspirations suggested by this service of consecration and com-

munion must not pass away barren and unfruitful ; but must be shown forth in a more
faithful life, a more gentle spirit. Christ
has Himself told us how we may most surely
manifest our love to Him : "Inasmuch as
ye have done it unto one of the least of
these My brethren, ye have done it unto
Me." Our love, our toil, our service must
be given freely and unreservedly, both in
the homes where God has placed us, and
in the world ; wherever sorrow or sadness,
sin or misery can be comforted or helped,
by our influence. And while we suffer
"for the sake of others," Christ Himself
will accept our services.

We come now to the Communion of
the Lord's Supper, seeing that it is no mystical rite, no miraculous sacrament ; it
binds us to no written creed ; it admits us
to no inner Church ; it announces no at-
tainment of holiness ; but it brings to our
remembrance the realities of our dearest
faith, and it is the symbol of the life we

desire to lead, as children of God, and disciples of His Son, Jesus Christ our Lord.

O Father, we come to Thee now, in deep humility. Thou hast led us to this hour ; send down now Thy Holy Spirit into our hearts, we beseech Thee ; that feeling Thy Presence, and knowing Thy Love, we may be kept very near to Thee, nor wander from Thee any more. We desire to consecrate ourselves to Thee, now and for ever. Give us Thy Grace to repent, and to leave our sins. Sanctify and amend whatever of good Thou hast given us, that we may be more worthy to serve Thee. May we so look to Christ, and try to follow Him, that we may become more truly Thy children. Keep us, O our Father, evermore in the knowledge and love of Jesus Christ our Lord. Amen.

We have pledged a solemn vow,
We are Christ's own liegemen now
Come or peril, woe, or loss,
We have taken up the Cross :

Never may we lay it down
Till death brings the victor's crown ;
And, from taint of falsehood clear,
"Bravely done !" with joy we hear.

Gaskell.

CHAPTER VIII.

SELF-SACRIFICE.

E come, therefore, to the celebration of the Lord's Supper, that we may bring ourselves into the presence of the Lord Christ, and feel the living touch of Him whose touch stopped the issues of sin. And in so doing, we take upon ourselves the pledge of Self-Renunciation. When we eat the bread and drink the wine, in confession before God that our Lord's spiritual meat and drink,—to do the will of His Father,—must be ours also, we lay our hands upon His Cross, and take it upon us. We come, not as professing to have attained to any worthy measure of the Master's Self-Sacrifice and Obedience, but as well knowing that we have it not ; not as having it but as desiring it ; not as claiming fellowship of life, communion of temper and of will with the Son of God, but to learn more and more of our spiritual poverty, that God in Christ may make us rich,—to know more and more of our soul's darkness, that God in Christ may give us light.

There is a Roman legend, that St. Peter the night before his martyrdom fled in terror,—that in the dawn of the morning he met our Lord walking towards the city with naked, bleeding feet, and stayed Him with the question, " Lord, whither goest Thou ? " and received the answer, with the awful "look" from the eyes of Christ he once before had met, " I go to Rome to be crucified again, in thy stead,"—and that the Apostle bowed his head in shame, and took courage, and returned, and witnessed a good confession.

The story is a fiction, but the lesson is
as the appeal of Christ Himself; for as
often as we refuse the cup, or the cross,
nay, far less than these, the thorn, the
scoff, the blow, the humiliation of a lowly
place before the World,—as often as we are
in despair of men, or in distrust of God,—
as often as the mortal burden so weighs
upon our hearts that the springs of faith
and love are crushed,—when the outward
circumstance subdues the inner life,—still
more, when we fall down in sin under a
temptation, and dishonour a conviction of
our souls,—what is this but to put our Lord
to shame, and crucify the Son of God afresh?
And here, before us, in the Lord's Supper,
are the Emblems of our peril and of our
strength, the weakness of the flesh, and
martyrs' blood; through these the Garden
scene, the prayers of Gethsemane, are renewed; in these we discern our Lord
apparelling his own soul for trial, and hear
the words as spoken to ourselves, " What!

can you not watch with me one hour! Watch and pray! the spirit indeed is willing, but the flesh is weak."

The moment our Lord specially selected for us, in which to unite ourselves to Him, was also the moment in which He Himself was most perfectly united to His Father, the moment when His own Self-Renunciation reached its highest point, and the whole spirit of His being was put first into Prayer and then into Deed, " Father, not My will, but Thine, be done." When there is no *Self*-will in us, there is one Spirit in God and Man. These were ever the moments in which the Father acknowledged the Son : in the humility and consecration of the Baptism : in the divine self-surrender of the Temptation : on the Mount of Transfiguration, contemplating the decease He must accomplish at Jerusalem : in the tremblings of self-distrust subdued by the prayer of Faith, the midnight gaze into the Face of God: in the preparations of the

Garden : in the consummating act on the Cross :—these were the times which the Father chose, to give divine attestations to His holy Child ;—and when we participate in the life of such moments we have fellowship with the Father and with the Son. It is in the critical times when the stress of duty, the trial of faith, falls most heavily,—the moment in which our besetting sin approaches near, in which if we keep the whole law and offend in the one point at which *our* will strives with God, we are guilty of all,—that through these great symbols we hear the Master's voice, " Remember *Me*,"—the body and the blood of Christ proclaiming, " If any one would be My Disciple, let him take up his Cross and follow Me."

There is another legend that speaks to us of a kindred truth. It tells us how,—when men's hearts were first kindled by the thought that the Lord's enemies possessed the Holy Places where He had lived and

died,—a band of religious Knights set forth
to seek for, and recover, the Cup into which
Christ had poured the wine at the Last
Supper.   It tells us how one of these, after
long and fruitless search, came back, worn
out and grey, to find another heir established
in his home.   And now in the cold winter-
time, he sat without "his own hard gate,"
dreaming of the light and warmth of the
sunnier lands from which he had just returned.   Suddenly he was startled by seeing
close beside him the loathsome form of a
leper, who begged from him an alms.   In
deep humility the knight remembered the
old pride with which, as he first set forth
upon his search, he had thrown an alms to
a leper, who then, as now, stood before his
gate.   He parted in twain the single crust
that remained to him, he broke the ice of
the stream that flowed by him, and he gave
the leper to eat and to drink.   Then he
looked up, and lo! not the leper, but the
Lord Christ Himself stood before him—

And the voice that was calmer than silence said :
"Lo, it is I, be not afraid !
In many climes, without avail,
Thou hast spent thy life for the Holy Grail ;
Behold, it is here,—this cup that thou
Didst fill at the streamlet for Me but now ;
This crust is My body broken for thee,
This water His blood that died on the tree ;
The Holy Supper is kept indeed,
In whatso we share with another's need,—
Not that which we give, but what we share,—
For the gift without the giver is bare ;
Who bestows himself with his alms feeds three—
Himself, his hungering neighbour, and Me." *

Thus may we too find our Lord ; our
daily lives, our commonest work, sanctified
and transfigured by the Obedience and the
Sacrifice which we take up into our hearts
as we draw near the Table of our Lord,
and lay our hands upon these Symbols,
will keep us for ever with Him in the
Presence of our God.

Oh God, Who hast given to us the example of our dear Lord Christ, to lead us
unto Thee, so pour into our hearts the

* (From "The Vision of Sir Launfal" by J. R. Lowell.)

Spirit of His Grace, we beseech Thee, that being made one with Him in Obedience and in Sacrifice, we may become one with Thee, even as He is one. Keep us, O Father, ever as Thy children, and as disciples of Thy Son, Jesus Christ our Lord. Amen.

> We covenant with hand and heart
>   To follow Christ, our Lord ;
> With world, and sin, and self to part,
>   And to obey His word :
> To love each other heartily,
>   In truth and in sincerity ;
> And under Cross, reproach and shame
>   To glorify His Holy name.
>
>   *Moravian.*

www.ingramcontent.com/pod-product-compliance
Lightning Source LLC
Chambersburg PA
CBHW020314090426
42735CB00009B/1335